When it wants
to scare another
creature, the
Australian
frilled lizard
pops up its
collar and
hisses.

The yellow-bellied sea snake uses its tail like a

paddle,

moving it side to side

while zooming

through the water.

With its flat shell, the African pancake tortoise can squeeze into tiny spaces out of its enemies' reach.

Alligators' mouths are very large.

Some alligators grow more than forty sets of teeth

in a lifetime.

Rattlesnakes can move very fast in warm weather.

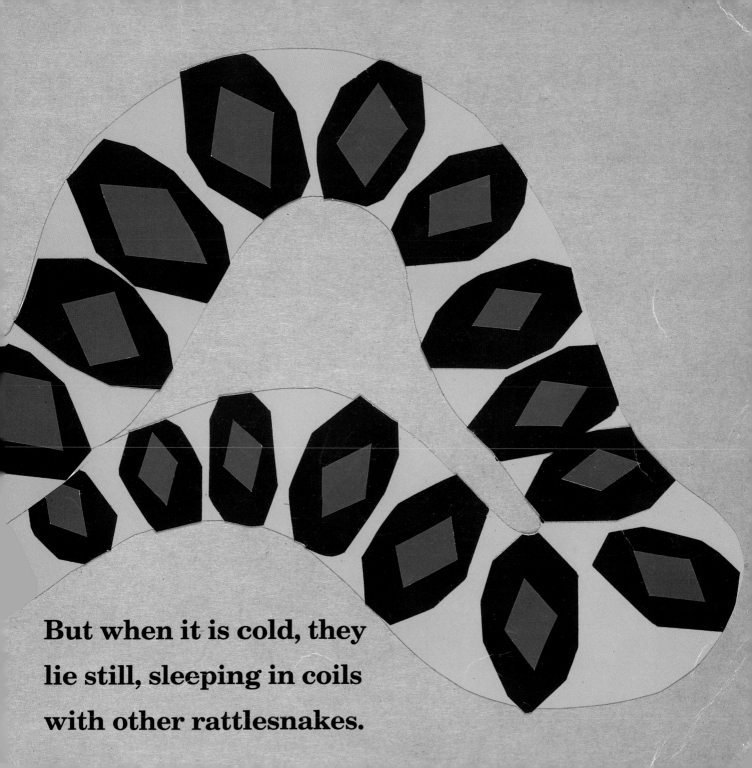

But when it is cold, they
lie still, sleeping in coils
with other rattlesnakes.

A Jackson's chameleon changes quickly
from green to yellow to brown as it

moves from leafy branches to bare branches.
Its tongue is nearly as long as its body.

Tuataras have lived along rocky shores
and cliffs for 140 million years,
since the time of the dinosaurs.

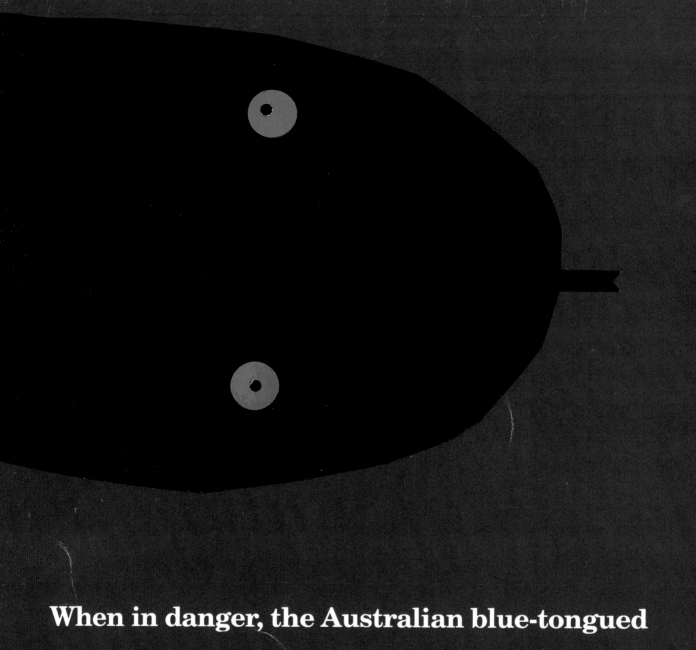

When in danger, the Australian blue-tongued skink puffs up its body, opens its mouth wide, thrusts out its bright tongue, and hisses.

The matamata waits quietly
in the water until a fish
rushes by, then it stretches
out its accordion neck
and snaps up dinner with
its big mouth.

The vine snake is hard to see as it waits for its prey.

Lying still on the branch of a tree,
it looks just like a vine.

The Komodo dragon is the largest lizard
in the world. It has poor eyesight but can smell
its dinner of goats or buffalo miles away.

Most land turtles move slowly, but the enormous sea turtle is a speedy swimmer and can move as fast as twenty miles per hour.

The yellow-headed gecko
has hooklike ridges
on its feet so it can
climb up trees, rocks,
or even glass.

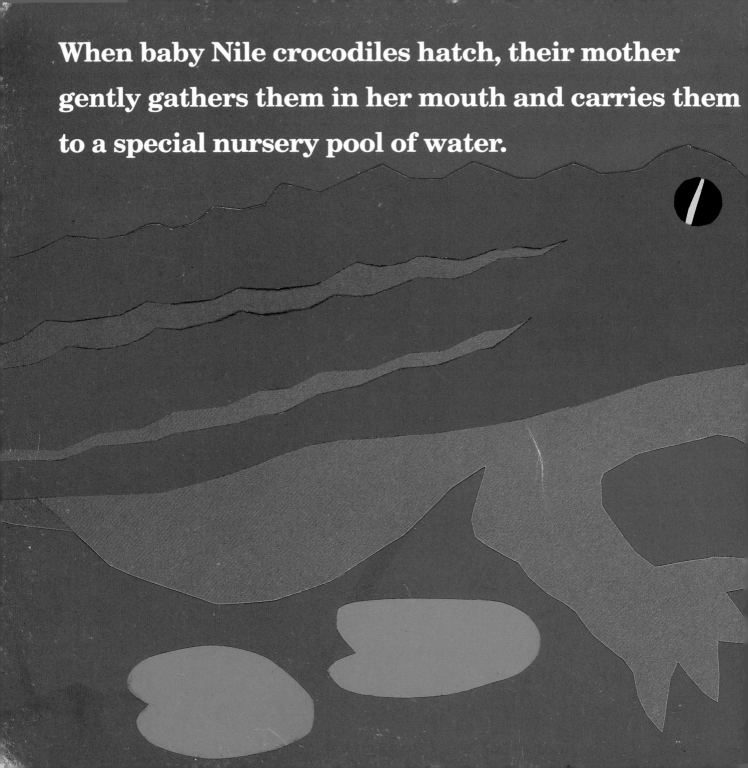

When baby Nile crocodiles hatch, their mother gently gathers them in her mouth and carries them to a special nursery pool of water.

Glass snakes are able to break off sections of their tails and slip away when they are in danger.